Windows into the Past for the Camera Shy

By

David Greshel

© copyright 2012 David Greshel
A Neon Sunrise Publication

Introduction

It's 2:30 AM and the restlessness begins to take over. I want to crash into bed and sleep through the darkened hours like most "normal" people but there's something that just doesn't want to let me get there. It's the same thing that has pulled me from deep dreams into wide eyed awake at 5 AM before the sun begins to creep over the horizon. That moment of inspiration, when the muse settles in and practically knocks me over screaming and will not rest until the creative urge has been satisfied. I love those moments...even if there might be times I wish the muse was more fond of daylight hours.

What you are holding now is a collection of those inspired times that reach back throughout my own personal history. I wrote some of these stretching as far back as high school and as recently as last month. It felt somewhat daunting to sift through the amount of material I've done to decide what I really wanted to share with the world. Some of those earliest works are a crude attempt; and while part of me wanted to share it all, the rest of me is content to leave them in the notebooks of the deep dark past. They were my catharsis and an outlet for emotions that I had a hard time expressing any other way, and it's better that they remain so. Writing is still cathartic for me now but I have a much easier time sharing those emotions these days.

The other reason it was somewhat of a task to go through the material is the fact that I would write on whatever was available if I didn't have regular paper close by. Envelopes, petition postcards, napkins, menus, church bulletins, blank time cards, magnetic poetry kits, and classroom whiteboards were all fair game and it was fun to revisit those physical artifacts. I never really know when something might inspire me to sit down and write so it has never hurt to be adaptable to the surroundings at hand.

So now the collection. What I most hope with this is the same thing I've always hoped when it comes to my writing – That it means something. Not just what I might have been thinking when I wrote it, but that it means something to you and that you find enjoyment in the time you spend reading it. I really can't ask for anything more.

I would like to recognize and thank a few people who helped make this possible:

First and foremost, God our creator - where all desire to create ultimately comes from.

My Grandmothers Barbara Bice and Evelyn Greshel – for having been a first inspiration as a writer and for instilling in me a love of reading at an early age.

My Family and Friends – for their encouragement and support, and for putting up with me when I throw random material at them and ask for feedback.

My Literary and Musical heroes who taught me to dream and to not be afraid to take a chance and put something together on my own.

It's been a long strange trip so far...but it still feels like only the beginning.

See you where the sidewalk ends...

David
3:30 AM
April 1st, 2012

Titled Works

Lunar Lullaby

There was an ocean between us
Deep blue and black rippling and rolling in endless cycles
As the saltwater foam slid along the rising shoreline kissing our toes
And beckoned back out towards the horizon that held our longing gaze
Still the spark within does not dim
Rather smolders and flickers like fireflies at dusk in early summer
Their soft light winking and fluttering in the open air
As the stars awaken from their daily slumber
And the moon begins her journey into the sanguine night
I watched the growing illumination of the heavens
Tracing familiar constellation patterns and inventing new ones
Searching for comet tails and falling embers to wish upon
That might envelope the passion and diminish the distance
That's ever present across the tides
A smile curls my lips as I close my eyes and drift towards
A slumber of my own
Knowing that you too have scanned the skies with a shared desire
And will soon find rest for a weary heart
Waking in an ethereal realm
Where there is an ocean between us
No more…

The Cycle of Life

I. Birth

Swirling darkness
feeding on the nurturing
of an unseen face
experiencing the joy
of an anxious woman
never met
riding for nine months
in the claustrophobic space
of a new mother's womb
feeding on her emotions
and split second cravings
through an intertwining cord
the only lifeline
for a tiny growing boy

Something broken

"how far to the hospital?"

screaming

"give me the drugs!!"
"bad for the baby"

squeezing

"push..."

unprintable comments

swimming towards the light
I don't want to leave

Light

thousands of tiny pinpricks
tormenting the eyes

crying

The first taste of life outside
the cycle begun

II. Childhood

"WAKE UP IT'S SATURDAY!!"
"honey..it's five thirty..."
"I DON'T CARE..C'MON LET'S GO!!"
"honey..let mommy sleep..."
"OH..OKAY MOMMY!!"
"thanks honey..."
"WHEEEEEEE!!!"

Cartoons and coco puffs
on early Saturday mornings
living innocent lives on the edge
with manic depressive mothers
reaching for an
empty jar of lithium
or the satin pillow
on the queensize bed

Early summer afternoons
skipping rocks
on the antique millhouse pond
playing barefoot in the sand
catching bullfrogs
and grass snakes
waiting for a chance
to scare Susie Gates

"honey..it's time for your bath..."
"NOOOOO! I DON'T WANT ONE!!"
"c'mon honey..don't give mommy a hard time..."
"NNOOOO! PLEASE!!"
"no it's time for your bath..."
"PLEASE MOMMY NOT TONIGHT!!"
"I'm sorry..."
"NOOOOOOOOOOO!!!"

First day of school
traumatized for life?
Or just initial
five year old shock?
The playground, cookies
milk and a nap

nap? Who wants
one of those?
The teacher is very nice
in an Adolf Hitler
sort of way
though we do wish
she'd shave that mustache
time to go home
thought we'd never leave
what?
We have to come back tomorrow?

The bus ride
a memorable trip
bouncing along
in the old yellow wreck
wondering just
whose seat would go next
and the driver
boy is that a scary thought
she left her curlers in
and her bathrobe on
we still wonder
what planet she's from

Home at last
turn the TV on
it's time for Sesame Street

On second thought
let's play outside
instead
we'll run around in circles
'til we feel dizzy
sick and dead

Bedtime
travels to storybook land
on the wind currents
of imagination
where dreams become nightmares
and nightmares become reality
keep the baseball bat handy
there are monsters
under this bed

Nightfall

Light fails and darkness wakes
rising to begin its sojourn
in the land of life
seeping into the shadows
and reigning the hours
which few dare inhabit
and there you'll find me
walking towards the meeting place
of land and sky
where the moon sits watching
and waiting for brother sunshine
to drive him from his perch

what is it to fear the creatures
of the night who are only animals
of a different shade
inhabitants of another walk of existence
and what of us who walk between
wanderers of time and space
light and dark
only shades that define
our choices

so rest happily
in your nightfall slumber
I call the wolf brother
await the rise of
our friend moon
and court slumber at
the dawning of the sun

If This Be A Garden

The shafts of light streaming
from the rising spring time sun
fell around me
in gradually increasing attempts
to invade my eyelids and end
this peaceful slumber
A yawn escapes as my lips
creak apart
sleep still trying to
maintain its grip
slowly vision sharpens
in focus

How many years have I lain here?

That above my head
a mighty tree has risen
arms spread out
thick limbs interwoven
with slender branches
fanned like foliage
covered tendrils
a singular canopy
filling the skyline
leaving just space enough
for the warmth
of solar illumination
to peek through

The next bit of oddity
creeps into my sight
as the shifting hues
begin to register
and invoke a sense of wonderment
as the soft blades of grass
reflect a periwinkle tint
and the amber colored leaves
shimmer on violet branches
and rustle in the light breeze
swirling through the maze of limbs
faintly reminiscing
an infant lullaby

Wanting to shake
the last vestiges of sleep
from this frame
I stand and rest a hand
on the massive trunk
eyes keyed to
coursing veins
that crisscross the entirety
of its surface
a pulse emanating
through my skin
and I wonder
if I lean in close
press my ear to the
slick purple haze
will the sound of
its thundering palpitations
overwhelm me?

Not but a moment passed
my thoughts fixated
on a topiary heartbeat
when the ground beneath me
begins to rumble slightly
and sprawling knotted roots
writhe and rise
climbing free of their
fertile dwelling

staggering backward
gaze transfixed in disbelief
as the mammoth sentry
slowly stretched its limbs
and emitted the unmistakable
sound of an audible sigh
and began to lazily amble
in the pathway of the sun

Shaking off the momentary paralysis
stepping forward to peer into the hollow left
in the absence of the tree
the light failing to pierce the darkness
completely
loose soil shifting beneath my weight
and I tumble
like Alice
down the rabbit hole

No end in sight
and light now absent
am I really falling
or has the world
just stopped moving?

Eyelids snap open
and reality reasserts itself
the pieces of a dream
crumbling away

How long have I lain here?

"The inner conversation goes like this..."

Set me up
watch me fall
you enjoy this too much

Black heart speak
can you love me?

Dark laughter
mocking
intentions are misleading
every inclination
screams in spite
self elevation
is the only purpose
left to these
suicide devices
looking for the signs
of light

Black heart
can you hear me?

Hide in your shadows
night won't last
forever...

<u>"Is anyone listening?"</u>

It floats just
beyond my grasp
the answer
I'm desperately seeking

Am I asking too much
that it never seems
to come within reach?
taunting my eyes
I can taste it
on my lips

Smaller thoughts
cascade quietly
beneath the louder demands
of pride
gentle whispers
*"you're not ready
for the responsibility
that comes with
the knowledge you seek...."*

...Drowned in the clamor of myself

"(Working Title)"

Feel this burning
stripping my skin
take over
where my blisters end
and bathe in these
flames

second coming
second birth

"in my defense..."

pretend to see
with hollow eyes
empty sockets
obvious to everyone
but me
yet no one wants
to say a word
afraid to speak
and maybe be cut down
bliss is sometimes
found in silence
so walk on by
walk on me
you're not really blind
if no one tells you
how to see...

"halfway there"

learn when
to say never
and find
a freedom
I've yet to embrace
wait for the heart
to acknowledge
the promises spilling
from lips
not known for their
follow through
latest in a long line of repeat offenses
far from
being the end
here I go again...

Pinpoints of Enlightenment

I remember a child
who dreamed of
chasing falling stars
across the darkened canopy
of the warmest summer night
wondering if angels
missed these glowing rays
as they plummeted
to dance on the desert floor
and finally rest
near the midnight blossoms
dying embers birthing
unfolding petals
as the child
becomes a man
who remembers a child
that dreamed…

Starving for a Second Opinion

The smallest part
always seems to
get in the way
sidestepping the tree trunk
to trip over a twig
content to pass over the obvious
in search of obscure rationale
to this plight
of my own making
look through me
and see this
for what it is
because I can't see myself
in this neverending story
lost in the plot
of my own self styled dreams

The Band Plays On

Footsteps crunch
in the fresh fallen snow
as I watch a world
marching to the chorus
of the damned
shuffling in time
to the numbing monotony
of the piper's dance

I shake my head
and turn my back
walking determinedly
the other way
listening to the sounds
of a different beat
and singing a hopeful song
smiling at those I pass
and beckoning them
to follow
and join the troupe
marching to the halls
of the king

American Child

Just to see you
makes me smile
A life begun
without a hint
of pain

Too bad it has
to end

It's a shame
you have to know this
but survival is
a dependent offspring
of necessity

see
life's a funny thing
it destroys
what it creates
with never a care
or concern

and today
you join the rest of us
in this sad mockery
we consider living
we stand on the backs
of the bruised
to claim another rung
on this ladder
of destiny
our selfishness
is only limited
to the span
of our reach

One day you'll awaken
without a thought
of happiness
but for now just smile

you won't know that bliss
for long

The Latest Fashion

Sometimes I just don't get
the things you want
the ideas that bounce across
your mind
in response to the things I do

Cause I'm scuba diving in a bucket
in search of some meaning from you
swimming in a glass of water
to understand this point of view
you cling to

What does it take
for a blind man to see
or a rich man
to give?

Maybe it would be better
if I knew exactly
what it is I want to say

or maybe I'll just
ask you
since you seem
to know anyway

Shadows

I can't remember how long
I've been wandering
in this valley of shadows
but it's getting colder here
My feet are bleeding
raw from this
snow and ice
footprints marked for miles
in crimson stains

How much further
do I have to walk
in this presence
of Death?
Cause I can't see
the path before me
and the wind is screaming
its tortured cry
in my ears
numb and burning

I wish I knew
what I did to get here
and how I'll figure out
why I'm wandering at all

but I can't worry about that now
it's not my place
I just have to keep trudging on
barefoot and bleeding
and allow God
to bring me through this
for the mountain
is close at hand

but it's surrounded by souls
screaming for relief
from this story of silence

Today

today is something strange
a passing moment
in a greater existence
that I haven't yet
begun to understand

ah, but I'm not promised
tomorrow
and I can't get back
to yesterday
I guess all I can do
is live in today

As I stand here
on the edge
of forever
hung somewhere between
heaven and hell
I wonder if
I was all
I was supposed to be
I can't get back
to yesterday
and tomorrow's too far away

Broken

I can't see why you left
or why I didn't see it coming
but I wonder
do you remember
the first time we met
in the halls of that hated high school
how I tripped over your books
and broke my wrist?
You were so embarrassed
and afraid
ranting and raving all the way
to the hospital
about insurance...
and what your parents might say

I was too numb
from staring into the brilliance
radiating from your eyes
and listening to the
nervous excitement
flowing through your voice
to think of anything
intelligent to say

Do you remember
the days that followed
how we were inseparable
and content
with this love
born of my uncanny ability
to be a klutz?

How about the times
we shared at the dawning
of the sun
having never slept
or thought of doing so
those nights spent
lying in a mid-western
cornfield counting stars
and arguing over
which sex was from Mars?

Do you remember when
they put you six feet
into eternity
and the tears that filled
my heart but not my eyes?

Do you remember?

Maybe when you hold me again
in heaven you'll tell me

Electric Poet

It's hard to contain
this electricity
that flows through my veins
burning these words
on the page
birthing this idea
in the caverns of my head

Emotions sizzle and pop
snaking away
through this pen
to strike the death blow
to the reader's heart

poetry served hot
handle with care

Cause words kill
faster than an embolism
and an uncontrolled thought
can wreak havoc
on the playing field
of philosophical conspiracy

Time grows short
here in never never land
Electric Poet
gives birth
to this creature
of misinformed intent
breathing life into
Frankenstein lungs
with the scratch of his hand

What's the Name of this Song?

I'm sitting here
and I don't know anything
about myself today
can you tell me
the name of this song
that runs the course
of my head?
Cause the words
won't come to me

I suppose it's not that
important to you
but I feel salvation
floating around
in there

right behind my eyes
but I can't see it

just inside my ears
but I can't hear it

my tongue struggles
to form the phrases
and I can't comprehend
the meanings
so obvious to everyone else

I guess it doesn't matter
anyway
no one wants to even try
to explain this to me
I'll just walk around
in here beside my brain
an endless march
in search of freedom
that isn't free

a life
I don't need
to walk too far
to find

Fragmentations

Love
love is an
encompassing enigma
a game written
in blood

Today
today is the edge
of forever
a fleeting moment
balanced between
heaven and hell

Tango
we dance in the mists of time
twisting across
the mindscape of ecstasy
pausing only for a glance
at the passing horizons of humanity
til we rest in what
first gave man birth

Reality
reality is nothing more
than one man's
perception
of his potential surroundings
a view that shapes and shifts
between birth and death

Insanity
insanity is where
you go
when reality
loses meaning
a place we've all visited
at one time or another

what I seek I'm afraid to find

Isn't
it
obvious
to
you?

I died today
and eternity is waiting...
wish you were here

...and the rest is silence

Well Dressed Fallacy

These eyes don't want to see
that I'm only pretending
to live this life
wearing a suit of skin
to cover these reptilian scales
it's my disguise
and here's my little secret

I can see yours too

Even if you hide it better
our souls scream
for fulfillment
some sort of substance
to place
inside this hole
but everything we chase
all the things we seek
do nothing but
increase the decibels
to a deafening roar

I can't stand this constriction
much more
but I've found someone
who fixed my friend
maybe he'll fix us too

and the scales peel away

brand new

8 bit Wanderlust

Concrete surrounds
my existence
silicon and steel
vagabonds of technology
stranded in
structure and form
here am I
traversing the plane of the living
a wanderer
in the jungle
of progress
and advocate
of the advancement
of surroundings
while the body sits idle
its nature unchanged

and I wander on...

114

Too late
this time
and am I only
subject to
that failure
stuck somewhere
in between
the pride and the fall

far gone
and incomplete
a blackhole burning
too much is staked
on the actions
of my intentions

where do I stand
when I don't understand
the question
and my pedestal
is in need of occupation
by anyone else

thus the reduction
of me
and my misunderstood
quest for freedom

Heart Attack

To speak
something done
too often without thinking
words fly
and are these not as bullets
to the mind?

The power exists there
the ability
to drive nails
with carelessness

and I wonder
how many I've left hanging
behind me
Am I killer?
A murderer with words
as weapon of choice?

It's only the
firing mechanism
"from the darkness of the heart
the mouth speaks"

so the killer is me
or at least
it's my chest
it beats inside

Medusa Dancing

Dancing inside
spiraling away

across the landscape
of futile intelligence
nothing here
makes much sense
it's all just a babble of thought
a pile of jumbled
ideas

why is it this way?
Where is the coherence
I see inside
your mind?

Dancing inside
spiraling away

I'm floating through
this mass of dreams
and lies
while Medusa sways
beside me
eyes that stone
this presence of mind
yet this tango continues
and the snakes weave their magic
around my blackened heart
I know the steps
without thinking
yet I fight
every movement
this is not who I'm
supposed to be

Dancing inside
spiraling away

and I'm not
the only one
I see you all around me
hypnotized the same
following the piper
fighting hell all the way

Foregone Conclusions

All we are
is all we've never been
A shell of substance
not too far
from the way I feel
Is this my life
or just how I perceive
the aspects of living
this way that I've
been taught
but haven't really
let saturate
the wellsprings
of my soul
the ongoing circle
of my realization
all we are
is all we've never been...

Lullaby

When the day is finally
laid to rest
and the stars
come out to play
just close your eyes
and lay here beside me
I'll sing you the world
on a string

Rest in me little angel
and don't you cry
I'll be here to hold you
when the night seems
to last far too long

But for now just rest
and dry all your tears
you can reach out
I'll catch you
and hold you
til morning comes
wandering wistfully by

20 Questions of the Soul

These strange days
that bleed into
twisted nights
will they contaminate my soul?
Or will they only serve
to mask the pain I cause...
at least until the headache comes

Can I breathe beyond here?
And what of my body's
eternal rest?
Will the mockery of the flesh
be complete?

Then let it be so
to each his own
and anything else
that will help me
ignore God
sneaking up behind
ever so present

What will it take?
I can't find you
weren't you my friend
or was that your little joke too?

Assisted
Self Inflicted

So I'm wrong

Please save me from me

Maybe a little liquid courage...

Too much to say
with so very little in the way
of speaking what I really feel
to you

Stumbling over my tongue
as it sticks fast
to the roof of my mouth
eyes glued to my toes
digging in the dirt
so lost in this beauty
before me
who wonders
whether I can even speak
at all
as she smiles
and walks on by

another chance
slips past
in the hourglass
of this dream
of you...

Chronos

Nothingness
cosmic beginnings unfold
in six days and a nap
the hourglass in motion
sand particles slipping
through a miniscule opening
a few grains at a time
taking forever
a priceless treasure

Racing
running against an opponent
I can't beat
in each passing moment
he takes another piece
of my life

Living
taking for granted
the thing I have the least of
final inhalations
of vital breath
quick death
no time left

O Father Time
I played this game
the one no man has won
But I never wanted Immortality
just eternity

Tapeworm

Is there anything at all
inside this attempt of mine
to avoid or destroy
your valley of flies?

Death
Decay
You're corrupting me

But have I ever really
tried to control you?
To lock these doors
that somehow appear
inside this weakness?

Just like a vampire
I invited you in
never to leave

Parasite

Malakoto's Dance

...and we dance
in the mists of
reality and nothingness
wondering what will happen
if the music ever stops
and we have to face the horror
of the silence once again
So we'll step in time
with good intent
while hoping for another round
to occupy
the dead space
between our thoughts
what to do
what to say
doesn't make much
difference anyway
cause we start again
to shuffle our feet
and swing our partners
round and round
praying for some reason
to speak our minds
to no one
and ask the hardest questions
to the thin air
stretching past our sight
alas, these thoughts that course
the movement of the ¾ rhythm
are lost in the white noise
of this soul experience
one to another
and we dance
in the mists of
reality and nothingness
wondering what will happen
if the music ever stops
and we have to face the horror
of the silence once again

Automatic

Savagery
Beauty
Civilized?
Welcome to real life
Is it fair?
Is it just?
Are you locked inside
reality with no escape
to your inner world?

I Find
I Lost
my mind
the other day
Helpless amongst friends
when I lived among the dead
in a life that wasn't mine

(dis)Orientation

Maybe I should
Just crawl inside
this shell that I call comfort
wrap myself up
in this blanket
of misnamed insecurities
and fade away
into the nothingness
that defines
this existence of fear

But what then
would I gain
from experiences
of victory
when I dwell in failure
and the misery
of anxiety?
Why should I try
if I can't get past
these feelings
of psychosomatic terror?

I can't do this

God help me

Sunrise To My Surprise

awakened to the prospect

of another day spent inventing

stories to entertain the subdued

remains of our tired relationships

but it's funny

how those vain imaginings

never seem to pass beneath

the shallow surface of a spoon fed understanding

only able to accept the trivial or mundane

still a small spark

pops in the wilderness

igniting a single flame

an idea glowing in eyes

that say more than your

words ever could

and I know somehow

the past will fade into a glimmering

pinpoint in the starfield

of this relational tapestry

woven between us

filling this view

sunrise to my surprise

seen for the first time

without the pretense

of what we might've meant

by that...

The Subtle Sting of Knowing

If you ever wondered
How many nights
Would end up this way
Would you have reconsidered
These decisions being made?

That's the thing about life
It never seems to wait
For a few moments to think
And we're left with the
Subtle sting of knowing
In hindsight
And there's enough teenage drama
To replace
A network soap opera

Still I see that look
In your eyes
When they come to you
With their latest dilemma
And I know that you'd
Love to just wish their tears away
But you share your own
And wrap them in your arms
Letting them know
The world will end up all right
Tonight

So just remember
You mean more to them
Then they ever really show
Especially at those times
When they really know
You were right
And they chose not to listen
To the wisdom of experience

Oh just one more thing
Before the curtain call
In case you haven't been told
I wish I had ten million friends
With hearts like yours
Worth more than gold

It would change the world...

The Last Spark Tonight

The bright lights downtown
Will shimmer in the hazy
Winter evening sky as the revelers
Clamor in the crowded streets
Near Times Square.
There will be many a sight to see
This new years rockin' eve
As the music enfolds them
and the dancing begins

Living life in this moment
A brief glance within the whirlwind
Different emotional snapshots
Still frames on a crowded page.
Like the couple idly strolling in the moonlight
Awaiting midnight's kiss
Or the laughter between friends at a bonfire
Remembering a weekend event.

A single teardrop stains
A pillowcase
As someone prepares to
Face a new year alone
Or the one a few blocks away
That tries to drown this year's troubles
In bourbon and beer.

All theses stories
Fill the bottom of the hourglass
As every grain passes through
We shake the etch-a-sketch
And start anew

So let the nakedness of birth remind us
God still dreams of Eden
So too the last spark tonight
Sets the flame for another chance
At making things right.

Love is Light

Simple phrases sometimes
Sound the best
In tangled situations
And I never met
A poet yet
That didn't err in favor
Of the sentimental
A time or two this year

Yet please don't think
I mean to excuse
These profound moments
That truth seeps through
The cracks of this
Hastily erected wall –
Love is like sunlight
Just a little touch
Is enough to kindle hope
In the dormant furnace
Of an icy heart

So raise a glass
Wipe the tears
As St. Valentine draws near
I'll be sharing a round
With Sgt. Pepper
While the Lonely Hearts Club band
Gets by with a little help
From my friends
And the world will be
Just like Heaven tonight

Genesis Daydream

I wandered in a daydream
And wondered at a field
Of fresh spring flowers
Waiting to emerge from
Winter's snowy grip

Just a dream and yet
I found myself entranced
Holding my breath as the first slivers
Of sunlight shattered
The cold darkness covering
This valley

Slowly, as the fiery orb
Rose higher in the morning sky,
Every flower yawned and swayed
Petals unfolding
Revealing nature's true beauty
Kept hidden 'til the promised
Season emerged

I smiled as the dream faded
And thought how similar
We can be
Our souls waiting to display
The true mystery
And love like light
Beckons us to unveil
Our own glory

And so it seems that I'm
Like Adam in slumber
Dreaming of Eve…

Knowing my friend
The Creator
Has fashioned someone
Just for me

Ethereal

We breathe in the essence
aloft in the waning summer breeze
the soft aroma enveloping us
slowly defining the very shape
of an unexpected moment
spent wondering just exactly
what it could all mean

There's a smile
briefly glimpsed
in the dying sunset
a growing indication
of the deepening emotion
corded and woven between us
revealing a storied tapestry
stretching out in all directions

The first stars arrive in the dusk
winking silver twilight
reflected in the soft pools of your eyes
their longing gaze hovering
in my vicinity
speaking in vibrant volumes
and drawing me within

I've run out of love songs
there are none left to play
no more clever harmonies
are necessary
since I found the perfect melody
you're the one I've been
looking for
from the very first day I learned
to sing

Light Years

If there was ever a reason
for self discovery
I had not discarded
I can't remember it now
There are no excuses
I haven't used
to try and bury this ideal
Suffocate & asphyxiate
this truth
yet I don't recall being happier
blind & bored
just unaware & unconcerned
The faintest glimmer changed everything
Beginning this awkward secret journey
plumbing the depths
of my stained consciousness
and awakening the revelation
that I never knew
the meaning of the darkness
until I truly saw the light

Secondhand Oasis

I watched it all crumble
and wondered why I never noticed
the sand that shifts around my feet
Strange how this temporary blindness
can hide this desert from me
I could've sworn this was a mountain
and yet this blistering breeze
has carried away every leg I thought to stand on
A whisper floats past
tickling my ear
and as I tilt to listen
eyes greet light
and the pain of true vision

So my world is falling down
soon to be a fading memory
But somehow it feels good to be a failure
otherwise there would be no second chances
no time to really see

Stained Glass

So often I ask myself
where the breaking point lies
How far I must endure
this overbearing charade
of a life I gave up living
Exhausted of trying to please
these dressed to kill hypocrites
and entombed spiritual midgets

Is the search still worth it?

White noise and hard rain
taunt my aching soul
beckoning toward a numbing oblivion
and yet something
buried deep within my still beating heart
screams for relief

Jesus where are you?
I was sure you'd be here
but all my pious exploration ever uncovered
was the ghost of your memory
I'm tired
but somehow still trusting
wanting to live
and You whisper
....Peace..Be Still....

Questioning the Stars

I sometimes speak to the midnight sky
wondering what weight words hold
in the expanse between
the stars & the sea
Do I speak in vain?
Are my heavenly inquiries
merely an exercise
in an unperceived futility?
These constant questions
crowd this fragile faith
I desperately cling to
in my burdened state of mind
Yet I am alive in the mystery
of it all
vitality streaming from the hidden things
Enlightenment is,
after all,
only possible if you're wondering at the darkness
wanting something more

Little White Lies

Is it really for the best
that I think everything is fine
when nothing works right
and I understand less
about the way things should be
the more I learn
how things are
I guess it's the lie I tell myself
to keep away from responsibilities
I don't want to accept
for actions I only wish
were someone else's
Regressing further into a logic
I pray will stave off
these barbarians at the gate
screaming insurrection
that makes a quickened pulse
course through me from this darkened heart
that knows what cruel logic won't admit
fall asleep and tell myself
It's all for the best

Fevered

Breathe
Take a chance and
inhale another moment of life
Please
I'm not ready to give in
and watch another slow procession
Breathe
Remember that there's more
than all that pulls you down
Please
I don't think this life
can be the same if you go
Breathe
You still have so much to do
so much worth experiencing
Please
I love you
just
Breathe

Lengthening Shadows

I wondered at
the substance of this life
moving forward
in a volatile environment
Am I just another blip
on the radar screen?
Or maybe a shadow
in this march of the walking dead
Is this it?
Am I content
to hide here from the light?
So I sit and ponder
until the last glimmer fades
and then doubt
that the light
was ever there at all

Behind the Curtain

Last in a long line
of repeat offenses
Struggle to contain the flames
that engulf my heart
Eyes go blind
in the inky darkness
alive in the palpitations
of this cruel rhythm
Every reaction
is the same as before
dance for the marionette
and wonder where the strings begin
ignorant of my own fingers
jerking me along

Inopportune Realization

Eyelids snap open to darkness
and claustrophobic tightness
limbs undone
breath ragged and in vain
skin brushing smooth alloy
so close on all sides
the horror of Amontillado

...Buried Alive...

A Specter Looks at a Century

Restless at the dying of the light
pulse quickening at the sound
of approaching night
but am I really alive?
or just a flashing apparition
illumined by the first slivers
of this full moon rising
stretching these ancient limbs
testing long held scars for meaning
Look into these eyes
Can you really see me?
or am I just imaginary...

...Raging Inside Me

I am living an
occupational hazard
this constant mixture
of darkness and light
An angel with the shadow
of a devil inside
stuck in a world of
cyclical behavior
Poster child for
a fucked up generation
First one to admit
I still don't know myself
at all

Magnetic #1

Above his need
was will over vision
language apparatus
am I mad?
Picture running water
languid delirious
together they scream
recall how I dream
summer symphony
would we stop
did we love
under enormous some
may manipulate
not to cry
crush their moment
sweat blood and ask me why

Magnetic #2

Chant at bitter death
black life drunk
love like summer
felt all these drive her
worship a moment
picture the diamonds
water light skin smell
lazy boy still here
after a thousand lies
blood from my sadness
together and delicate
ships stop vision
suited to power
bare arm sweat
void yet essential
I loved you
iron sky fall
friend recall
honey I sing
but I'm gone

Magnetic #3

Language like beauty
languid in sunshine
elaborate and produce
madmen stare at the moon
manipulate and incubate
whisper to the flood
road music trips me out
shadow symphony in winter wind
about a girl beneath sweet petals
dreams mean eternity
ask me sometime

Magnetic #4

Felt like I could
dream you and me together
languid beneath
this forest moon
chant away the blood lust
drunk on honey
essentially crushed
manipulated
asleep in the sun
pink rose petals
did bare love
let your light shine
delirious eternity sings
of delicate beauty
a moment gone
still I recall
spring and tiny water music
picture a thousand
I only need one
whisper it to me
love above all
worship through language
live today

Magnetic #5

Leave after asking
still I whisper
like a man without
eternity
summer never parts
showing only those
near the void
alive
elaborate from there
tell me how I was
dream and recall
this black flood like death
screaming within bitter moments
shadow language produces
a weak symphony
sordid and repulsive
I run to the rain
cool and delicate
enormous sun soars blue sky
time always sees
true vision

Inspirations

While a lot of the stuff that eventually makes it onto the page could be considered autobiographical, all of my writing has its inspiration somewhere and every artist searches for their muse.

The next section is made up of poems that I wrote specifically for someone or that were directly inspired by them or the events currently happening in their lives. I have opted not to call out who they were for so as not to take away from the reader being able to relate them to their own lives or experiences. Those folks who inspired these words will know which ones were theirs if they read this; and the words will always be meant for them even as I hope that they mean something special to everyone else that reads them now.

Chimeral Love

In pursuit of the
language of love
I've traveled many
tortuous miles
never freely given
hesitantly taken
I wonder if love
was worth the trip

I'm certain that
I love you
but unsure
if I'm right
you might just tell me
what I know
or the fact that I'm just crazy

Maybe I'm just
chasing chimeras
in pursuit of love
from you
maybe you can tell me
is it just
chimeral love?
Or is it
something more?

Dancing with the Infinite

I've often wondered what it's like
to dance before the throne
to hear what is said
in places that I've dared
not go

And I often wonder why we
keep pace with this life
that somehow drags and pulls
at the very nature of our existence

Can you tell me why you dance
flower child
Why you never seem to be affected
by this constant stream
of negativity
flowing from
mass media conceptions

Do you know where your love
comes from and what the substance
of joy is all about
cause I've never seen
a life like yours
innocent and carefree
the kind of life
I'd like to be

Can you teach me how to dance
flower child
in this life for the next
we'll enter the heavenly places
with a quickening flurry of steps

so as we draw to a close
is it true what's been said

"there are no strangers here
only friends we have not net"

if so then life is truly
more fun when we dance

Valentine

Today I stopped to watch
a budding rose unfold
in the new dawn sunrise
mesmerized by the careful
parting of petals
slowly reaching its complete
outstretched beauty
such a lovely sight
to ponder
as I turn to travel on

Turning to see you
standing in the sunlight
with a flower
of your own
and my heart matches the rhythm
of your steps
as the light sparkles
in your smiling eyes

flowering beauty is fleeting
when you're near
melting into
the landscape
as true beauty
treads its path

Alive in the Mystery

Sunshine melts
Away the expanse
Of this lazy
Winter day
Smiling at the
Memory of
A mountain sheathed
In cold ivory
Gliding by as the lift
Guided us to our
Anxious destination
Where the world
Unfolded beneath our feet
And I think I could've
Laid there in that
Powdered ice forever
If I knew that you'd be near
As long
And it wasn't daylight
That shone so bright
But your smile
And your laughter
That ignited the night

So what's the story
Morning glory?
Can you tell me
What your heart knows?

A new season
Begins in bloom
Filling the space between us
And what will this garden grow?
The slowly rising tide
Of this affection carries us aloft
In a mystery I'm enjoying
With a hope
That you feel the same…

The Fine Art of Grieving

Sometimes I think
These tears
Will never cease
That my eyes
Are destined to
Be fountains of sorrow
Vainly trying
To wash away this
Numbing pain within
My attention rising
To the even stars
As my mind and heart
Echo the singular
Question
Tearing from my lips
Between sobs

Why?
Why like this?

R.E.M. on the radio
"Everybody hurts...sometimes...
Everybody cries...sometimes..."
Doesn't help me
This time
And then the clouds
Spill over
Raindrops plummeting
Earthward
A small voice
Whispering in
My heart
And somehow I know
That God is crying too...
Arms wide open
Wanting to be my comfort
My abba father
If I would
Let Him

And I run to
Those arms
Hungering for the healing
Of this shaded pain...

A Scrapbook of Sorts

Lost in these
Pleasant memories
That could fill
A scrapbook of sorts
A story of laughter and good times
That are always near
Whenever you happen
To be here

The pages turn
Each one with
A smiling face
And angel eyes
That light up any life
They touch with
Infectious joy
That leaves no doubt
That you're "sooo excited"

And how could we live
Without knowing that
"Honeydew is such a cute name
For a watermelon"
Or that
"You were a great Beast"
Following after the
"Freeze dude"
(Iceman Sarah)

There may be
A presentation today
But I doubt we'd
Find you there,
Just remember you
Might have the same effect
"No I don't, Watch!"

What else can be said
Of this flower
In the oasis?
A bright spot of sunshine
In this cloudy existence
And a friend
We wouldn't trade
For the world
(Just remember… I'm not Steve)

It starts with a flicker...

Sometimes I wonder
What you must be thinking
When someone else's world
Is caving in around them

You're always the first one to listen
The one they run to when they
Just can't seem to work it out
And I know you wish that you could fix
Every heartache they face
But the grace you live is something
They need more than another band-aid solution

And this is how it begins
The path that has been chosen
Your love displayed is the spark in the darkness
It's in their eyes when they hear your counsel
The hope that starts with a flicker
Like a fresh lit candle flame fighting
Against the incoming winter breeze

So I wonder what thoughts
Run through your mind
For the thousandth time
When the heartache
Makes a repeat offense
And I smile
Knowing that your arms are open
In a comforting embrace

If it ever seemed like it went unnoticed
Like being the first one to listen
Last one to be heard
Know that you make a difference
Be it one life or a thousand
It starts with a flicker
One bright spot to start a flame...

"Tell me…"

It's funny sometimes
How two little words
Can send the mind into
A tailspin of over-activity
And imaginative scenarios
That could entertain the
Most spontaneous romantic

So what to tell you
What to tell you…

I was never sure
I'd heard an angel sing
'Til your voice filled my ears
In a love song sung for friends
To bless their wedding day

And Taboo's not really
Quite the same
When you're not
There with all
The clever answers

So put the windows down
And turn the stereo to eleven
"Hey isn't that our exit?"
Never worried for a moment

These tattoos are more
Than just skin and ink
Each one a story
A memory

Like words that still echo
From a Tuesday night concert
Hold that left ring finger high
And know what was spoken is true
This year's about falling in love
And we're holding on to our friends
With everything we've got…

For My Girl

I remember the first time
I ever saw your face
The way you smiled
And squinted in the hospital lights
When I held you baby girl
Made every painful hour
Worth taking

And who could forget
The very first time
You had a birthday cake
To celebrate a year of first steps
And first words
And first Christmas memories
I still love to see those photos and remember
The smile as you blew the candle out
Only to dig both hands in the cake
And giggle when the icing squished between
Your fingers

The years went so quickly
Seems like yesterday
That I took you to your first day of school
You were so brave and didn't cry
When I turned to go
And I loved your excitement when you
Came running to me at home
Time marches on
Never worrying itself on our passing events
So many firsts written on it's pages
First dance, first test, first kiss
I treasure up these memories
And smile when I think
Of the joy you've filled my life with

Then there's always the first time
You got to drive alone
Nervous doesn't even begin to describe
The anxious energy a mother feels
When their teenager is the one
Behind the wheel
You were so proud and excited
I was just relieved

I remember so vividly the night
The call came
And the way my heart crashed
When they told me to come down
Seems another's carelessness
Had taken my baby girl
And the tears ran like a torrent
As the rain washed my feeling away

Things are different these days
Where there once were the fragile dreams of
A love-struck teenage girl
Sits a vacant room
So many things I wanted to say
So much of life I was ready to share
So many memories that will
Never feel the same

Yet I will smile still
Even with the pain
Because I know that I will see
My baby girl again

An infinite sunrise

Awake in the night surrounding
These intimate encounters
Watching you there in my arms
And smiling as your warm breath tickles
Against my chest
Lightly brushing my fingertips
Along your temple
Smoothing away a curl
As I feel you shift and murmur softly

And I wonder if this is
Simply another apparition
Byproduct of a deepening slumber
Where I'll wake up and realize
That the comfort was
Just cotton and down
Sewn up and stuffed in
A matching sham
An inhabitant of a world
I can't seem to hold onto
Beyond the edges
Of the night

Small slivers of light
First glimpse of a summer sunrise
Catch my eyes as I turn
And watch the virgin rays
Cracking through the
Half drawn curtains
Looking back
Feeling your lips trailing tiny kisses
Along my chest
Your eyes blinking sleep
And sparkling in the half-light
Of this rising day
Loving the softness
Of your skin on mine
And the way your voice
Lilts in my ear

Holding this moment
And knowing that
It's more than just
A waking dream

Smiling in the light
Of an infinite sunrise
And wanting more
Than anything
To be enveloped
With you in this
Embrace
Alive in the glory
Of a love
I always hoped to find

A New Dawn

Snowfall in the starlight
Alive in the whisper of things
Dancing between us
In the midst of a half spoken dream
Breathing in sunlight

I wondered if I might've
Simply imagined the
This fragile state of being
A silken spiderweb
Cascading down the spires
Of a golden tower glistening
In the half light of dawn

And I saw you there
Fresh like the first blossoms
In spring unfolding to the
Growing warmth of the morning
Flashing a smile that would melt
The last vestiges of winter
Clinging to these shores

Is this a dream?
The idle fancy of a wandering heart?
The closer I get to this shimmering palace
The more I wonder at the possibility
Of a mirage...

All these things are swept aside
With the twinkle of your eyes
Coming to rest on mine
And I never heard the singing
Before now.....

The Chorus Goes like this

Something worth wondering
Is never thought
In vain
There's room for all
These things that
Often seem to pass
Behind these eyes
And wander deeper within
Like how that sweet smile
Lights up a room whenever
It curls your lips
Or if that sparkle
In your eyes
Lingers even when
They're closed
How the smile never
Leaves my lips every time
I hear your laughter
In my ears or the way
I know you grin when
The sass rolls off your tongue
More than just a passing
Fancy or an idle fascination
An underlying connection
That stretches between miles
And knowing that I wonder
Simply means this is only
The beginning
A song that's still being
Written and
You're the melody I've
Been dreaming of
Since the very first time
I sang….

More Than A Memory

Wistful wishes can't hold back the hands of time
that spin across the face of this dial and move us
forward across the days and months and years.
Like Frost we came to a fork in the road
and decisions have been made as to which is the better path
although opting for the less traveled route hasn't always
proved to be the wisest choice.
The miles stretch between us now and sometimes that
distance seems to be more than just geography
yet somehow there is more than a memory
that binds us when the light is fading to dusk.

Seasons come and pass
turning our thoughts to the simple joy
of these holidays we've always loved to share
knowing the bonds of family stretch farther than these
state lines could ever hope to dream.

The sands of time still slip through the hourglass
and the years march forward undeterred by the dreamers
looking for a chance to re-imagine days long past.
Phone calls and letters facilitate the majority
of our conversations as the months roll on
and the smiles always come when the talk turns to
holiday dinners and overdue visits.
We may not always get there
we may not always spend those days
in each others' company
but we're only as far away
as each others' thoughts and prayers
we're only as distant
as this hope inside our hearts
we're more than a treasured memory
we're an ever growing family
and our home is always near.

"Time keeps on slipping..."
funny how subjective that line tends to feel
when you're stuck on a crowded interstate
and the world starts to melt into one
continuous noise of idling engines and early spring showers
wishing you were driving for any other reason
than another trip to that hospital
full of sterile claustrophobia
and the lingering smell of poorly scented antiseptic

The subjectivity spins
and the line takes full meaning
as you try to squeeze every second
and give the hands on the clock a permanent vacation
longing for the sound of cold digital pings
to be replaced by the familiar twist and rattle
of a beloved gumball machine

"...into the future"
how long is that exactly?
How much do we have?
We're not promised tomorrow but we keep expecting
it to come around
one more day is one more chance
to live
to love
to laugh and share a smile
to keep fighting for the next one
and start all over again

still there seems to be a darkness
hovering on the edge
waiting to roll in and sweep it all away
remember two hands
clasped together
clinging to one another
a shaft of light shattering the black
hold on to that moment
and never let go
til the first rays of the new rising sun
come to warm you both

A Bolero's Spark

I saw the beginnings of a roaring flame
the smallest glimmer of a spark
within an aching heart
that speaks to you softly and begs for a moment of relief

that heart weighs heavy
amidst the ever present trials of life
and the sting of unrequited feelings
the need to be strong
and the drive to succeed

the spark sputters and grows
and a smile slowly appears
as a little boy's laughter & joy
creep into your view
infectious and amazing
the source of unquenchable determination
worth everything and more

These are the beginnings
once a glimmer now ablaze
the still beating heart of this beautiful woman
benevolent mother
loyal friend
someone foolish enough to walk away
hasn't truly seen her
or known how to see the spark
that's waiting to burn

I heard Buckley sing about a last goodbye
and thought of you
which struck me as odd in context
but brought a smile nonetheless
you're the last one I want to say goodbye to
and the first to fill my thoughts with hello

maybe that sounds too easy
just a little bit cliché
but then the simplest truths
are often taken so

a clever phrase or well placed word
that burst of enlightenment
that I've been searching for to illuminate
the thoughts I'm trying to portray for you
amid my own anxieties and neuroses
vainly trying to get my tongue to speak what
my mind and heart have entertained

how you're a delicate blossom
desperately waiting to bloom
fragile petals aching to unfold
and display the full beauty
that's been within you all along
heartbeat pulsing with quiet strength
steady rhythm building to a crescendo
that speaks to the passion you possess
and the love you dream of sharing

or how the light catches your eye just right
and your smile is just infectious and warm
with a laugh that's impossible not to share

all these things and more fill
a mental mixtape that never leaves
my stereo
flip and hit rewind
you're the song that's stuck in my head
the one I never want to forget
and I wonder if I might have this dance

Reflection of Another Morning

The sun begins to peek over the horizon
first rays of dawn stretching out
like fingers on outstretched hands
waving to greet the coming morning

I want to rise and smile
but there's a sudden rush of reality
that I'm faced with
a cold remembrance of what felt like a hazy dream
surely that's all it was...
right?
But those hours past creep back to the forefront
and I know it's true
Somehow though I never thought
it would be so soon that
I would have to see a morning break
where you wouldn't be there
to share it with me
that this would be a day
I couldn't dial you to talk things over
share a cup of coffee
or glass of wine
that it's really time to say goodbye...

Sitting here on the edge of the bed
watching a little one peacefully dreaming
and wondering if you did the same
when I was the one
so small but full of life
filling your days with smiles and laughter
and at times sighs and prayers for strength

the years flew by
full of firsts -
First steps...first days at school
first fights...first loves...
first broken hearts...
through it all we didn't always agree
but I never once doubted you loved me
I might not have always accepted that
and I'm sure that at those times
I knew it all
and when I finally figured out I didn't
you were always there to love me just the same

You always fought for us
lived each day to make a life for us
to keep our family strong
to give us the chance to grow
and become the beautiful people
you always knew we'd turn out to be

When you found out
that your own body was turning on you
I'm sure it would've been
so easy to give in
but that's not your style
and you never let it
get the best of you
living each day with full intent
squeezing out every last drop
you could

And then I do have a smile
remembering all these things
every lesson that you taught
intentional or not
you showed me what it means
to be strong
how to have a hope
to carry on

so if this is goodbye
then it's just
goodbye for now
and I know there will
be a day
someday
when we hold each other again...

Untitled Works

"Just like heaven..."
that's the line that always ends up
floating back to me
landing somewhere just this side
of trivial and not too far from jaded
last lesson in the misspent plans
of new romantics and fragile dreamers
wishing to find some lingering whisper
of hope in the arms of another soul
singing the same chorus back to them
out of reach and slightly out of key

This fairytale is not an abstract concept
or some undiscovered countryside
I know all the melodies and clever rhymes
and have maybe sang them for a few
a time or two today
but I only wanted to feel alive for the moment
I shared the skies

Still worth a smile to ponder
these thoughts that often
beg to wander through the
silent twilight hours when slumber
tends to loiter on the edge of rest
and casually flirts with the heavy notions
of what ifs and might've beens

First shards of dawn spill into the depths
beckoning towards the intangible moment
awakened in the warmth of renewal
and the resolution
that hope is never in vain
love is never wasted
and somewhere there is someone waiting
to say that you're just like heaven too

Sometimes I think of what it might mean
if I stepped outside of these ideas
I so often cling to
really stopped to examine it all
from more perspectives than
just my own
I wonder what implications
would stretch out and begin
to color this imagination
it was never yellow brick
and straight forward
never simple or absolute
but then if it were
I tend to think I would've
lost interest years ago
or just settled for complacency
and never opened the door again
is it better to remain within
the things you know?
To dwell only in the realms
with the boundaries we're
aware of?
If safety was the goal
the locks would never turn
we would never venture out
so the unknown beckons
enticing with what ifs and wonderment
I can't see the path but
I can see the stars
and the other space
the in-between place
it's calling in the half light
and all it takes to get there
is for me to just take one step...

We speak in dreams and memories...clever phrases hidden from the cold light of reality illuminating the landscape....it's not fear that keeps us there...more of a sense of belonging...it is who we are...the fantasies you cling to when life seems too hard to cope with....the fairy tales you treasured as a child...that other world where magic and true nobility are interwoven with the struggle to survive the tyranny of the ordinary and become something more than just a man...something you push aside in the daylight hours...choosing to believe what others perceive you are....living as though what they think truly defines who you are....returning to us only in the depths of slumber...and it's the only time you ever smile.....

I've watched this darkness for so long that it holds shapes and movements that would escape those huddling together around me. In fact they wouldn't even know that there's a difference...something out there that is waiting to challenge their blindness. A small flickering off in the distance that has been calling to me since it first caught me in its shining brilliance. That....light...stung and burned...yet I find myself wanting to return....to feel it cover my skin...it's hard to explain....but there was also this voice....
whispering...soothing....asking me to stay....I ran...back to the cover of this eternal dark...the cold comfort of familiarity....but it's still there...pricking the back of my mind...calling me to travel further in that small voice....and I want to go...but what I seek I'm afraid to find....afraid that when the veil is torn aside the reality of who I am will frighten the owner of the voice...and yet He calls...

...wild nights raging against the coming of the neon sunrise...drinks and laughter painting the atmosphere amid the pulsing rhythms floating from these speakers...and we danced til dawn...finding slumber beneath the glowing amber sky...encircled in the morning glory blooms unfolding to carry us home...

and so it came to pass that dreams were finally outlawed...regulated unconsciousness was enforced and overseen by the machines we built to help build a smarter planet for a better tomorrow....there are no more aimless wanderings inside the collected imagination...and we learned what it's like to be alive and dead in the same moment...for is it really living if there are no dreams to share? no secret places to disappear to?

Today is a
curious thing

it struggles
to remember
when was yesterday
but can't seem to
find the time
to wait
until tomorrow

Sometimes I have to ask
What I did to warrant this
Calamity that descended
Upon my life,
A drunken party crasher that never left
And stained a favorite carpet.

Do I really need another
Pop quiz on the state
Of my faith?

I want to trust that
There is nothing that I need
Nothing to concern myself over
And yet everyday reminds me that
These troubles are all I can
Seem to think about

I meant that prayer
That tumbled from my
Tired lips this morning when I
Told You that I would leave
All these things at Your feet
So how come I can't loosen my grip?

The radio hums softly
An old song filling the air
Reminding me that
"Everybody hurts…everybody cries…sometimes…"
And a small whisper
Just inside my mind
Asks me just to be still and know…

Still shadows often hide the smallest flicker of light
A spark that dances in defiance of the surrounding night
Like a falling star burning a path through the heavens
In search of the last resting place in the valley
Amidst the remains of the fragile souls
Lost and alone in the wandering night

I am alive in the possibility
Of all that could be
Unwilling to wonder what
Might've been
And coming to terms with
What is

To speak of the past
Is to filter the experience
Of the present
And prophesy of the future
In the absence of learning

To speak slow
that my mind
might blink
too far
so long
lost on you

watch the silhouette fade away to the inside of a distant shadow as we creep along the expanse of this haunted night.....footsteps tread lightly as we walk among the dwellings of the left behind....tension dimly lit by the last sliver of a dying moon....will the past undo the things we've often hoped for with their whispered resolutions and uncertain dreams....troubling this sleep we often never rest...compelled we wander on.....not quite lost but never really found....

a spirit dancing in the slender silver moonlight...awkwardly stumbling through the forest with the lonely creatures of the night....merely a specter haunting the shell of a former life....I am the ghost of a better tomorrow....the last vestige of a once vibrant heart now beating in time with the broken and spent....funny that it always seems to be me who never wants to see this transparency so evident to all these prying eyes....always quick to critique another and leave their own black hearts be....walk on by...walk on me.....this ghost remembers a life you can only dream....

speaking in shadows and bittersweet melodies....I thought I saw the faintest trace of a smile as this thought crossed your mind.....too bad we never got past the simple pleasantries of being alive and alone and I think I might want to take this back when all is said and done....my heart is the worst kind of weapon and it's pointed at another tragic fairytale that we somehow want to believe is the reality we both belong to.....nothing left now but the saddest words we've ever shared even though we never once said one phrase past hello....might've beens and should've dones are the only faint memory I'll want to have as the jukebox plays another lonesome tune and the world runs blue in the dark of this welcome night....

the softest speech sometimes stills this beating heart that jumps every time the shadow falls over the room where we often tend to find ourselves....alive in the last fleeting glimpse of sunset before the stars appear to illuminate the even sky...tiny diamonds that sparkle in the deepest indigo...and if we close our eyes this moment might freeze in time and suspend us evermore in this bliss we discovered in a passionate encounter....quick as it arrives it's gone and I'm left here in these sheets listening to the faintest whispers of the midnight breeze and wonder if it was nothing more than some elaborate dream....

...I thought I caught a flash of some memory we shared amidst the cold ashes of what once was a bonfire ablaze.....the flicker floats past....a vain glimmer of hope when none ever dared surface before....is it too much to ask....too much to think that maybe there was something more to who we thought we could be....an enigma within this mystery....smile now and remember me the way I was....I'll remember you as someone I used to know that's long since gone away....and the winter breeze will soon scatter these ashes....another funeral at sea....

I walked over these streets...dimly lit and shadowed in the presence of the fast approaching winter chill....wondering if the world might stop for me if I asked nicely....intent on breathing in the last remnants of autumn still hanging in the breeze....smiling sadly at the thought of you and where you might have wandered off to....chasing those things that never really satisfy you in the end....the moonlight pierces the shrinking shadows receding from the rising tide of silence....broken by the song of a new dawn approaching and the hope of spring and your return.....

speak to me in riddles and I'll answer with enigmas....it's never just the edge of night but a fine line drawn over the sand of this desert I lived in once upon a time....the chill seeping into the dry breeze that swept through me in the dead of some winter life....I only wanted to see the sea again...feel the salt sting my eyes and the waves crash around....I only wanted to see the ocean come to terms with who I wanted to be....a lost soul floating on the reef in search of another song to sing.....

....wonder if the daydream is as good as the memory...standing on the water's edge watching the foam rush between my toes....warm salt in the breeze invading my senses....smiling at the thought that I might see the sunrise in your eyes....the golden rays that glitter in the swelling seas....one blink and the rest is just a fading outline...a blur in some flickering reel as the film spins at its end....did we ever even stand there....did the sun rise at all......sometimes it's best not to wonder....and let the band play on......

stars in flight...first one seen tonight...watching the tail stream across the dark...illuminating the brilliance already shining in your eyes...twinkling in the descent...smiling as it lands...a glittering jewel dancing in your hand...wish for more than just one night...believe we're alive and awake in each others' arms...enraptured in this kiss....

Sun spots
burn retinas
to small dots
as daylight
drowns the darkness
and morning
bleeds to life

remember like it happened
just an hour past
I sold Paradise
for an apple
to a devil
in a snakeskin suit

Is there anything at all
that doesn't make you
want to break down
in a million pieces?

I know that it's
not what you thought
it would be
but no one said
this was easy

or did you think
that everyone
would bow down to you
like a queen?

I sometimes wonder if I might convince the world to change if I stop just long enough to stare inside this fragile breath that heaves within my chest and see that it doesn't depend on me to keep time with the rhythm of this heart that pulses and pounds in a sound of music that emanates from the very fabric of being. But being is such a loaded position that offers more complex questions than simple solutions and doesn't seem to mind this orientation of a slightly amusing dichotomy, and I think therefore I am all the more unwound and high strung along the tightrope of philosophical musings and spiritual undertones. To this end it may seem that all we aspire to is simply a flash of smoke and mirrors aimed at concealing the unappealing reality that nothing natural is ever enough to quell the mounting urges that whisper there has to be more than this but given time this fancy too will pass. After all I'm happier here in the dark when there's no one to remind me of the light yet I sometimes wonder if I might convince myself to change if I would stop just long enough to really be...

Imagination rambles in a sort of time stream of consciousness that is not quite aware of the myriad hallucinations floating on the sailing sea in memory and afterthought astronaut flight in this outdated starflyer strapped to a scrap heap and burning in the late summer afternoon when I lost it all amidst the piles of unanswered postcards from another season of life in the valley of the shadow of dismay at the fact that I've made so little progress away from the winter of eternal conflict threatening to envelope everything I hold dear abby I can't seem to make up your mind when it doesn't matter anymore that we'll never have Paris between us she's way too high to notice that the view from Venus is rather jaded and she can't abide Mars and all his wandering ways to skin a cat there's more than I can say and less that means anything to you assuming everything ariel dances in my room and looks could kill when I dress to impress or forget to pay the rent and end up living on a freeway listening to signs and driving by feel this way again when I taste your lips against mine in the only kiss I ever want to know when I lose the only heart I have to give it away in the whispering wind where my lady's stairway lies and makes this world an illusory place where you have to understand the dream is over and out we've got ourselves a convoy rubber duck there's a phone call aimed at me tonight is something I just don't have the stomach to face up to in the morning when there's nothing left to say but I loved you and wonder where you might've run to...

I only wanted to see the sea one last time
A lazy thought that floats on the edge of my consciousness
fading with the years and amusing memories
how long has it been?
since I last felt the undulating foam tickling my toes
or tasted the brine on the ever present breeze
seems like a lifetime has passed
wandering in search of one more clever rhyme
and maybe a shot of Cuervo with a little salt and lime
idle fancies never do run dry
their easy reach enough to quell the longing
that sometimes whispers in the faint evening light
that there was something lost in all this aimless movement
soft and barely spoken
but still enough to bring a smile
The melody rising til there's nothing left
but to sing along and remember
that I only wanted to see the sea...

Daydreams and memories
are all that's left
of you now

It's a shame you left
so soon
I might've told you
what you meant
to my point of view
how much your being here
kept me in a solid state

But no
you were never sure
of what life meant to you
of what my presence did
to your state of mind

Did you ever see
how much I loved you?

Did you even care?

Perhaps it's best
that daydreams
and memories
are all that's left
of you now

I always seem
to walk in for the credits
and turn the radio dial
to the end of my favorite song

behind
forever behind

but then dreamers
always are

residents of another realm of space
reminders of a forgotten time

Stolen dreams unfold
in the heart of desires
unmet in the light

I wanted it
it wanted me more

nonstop
unwelcome in the face
of an uncontrolled
state of being

I wanted it
it wanted me more

too much comes
overwhelmed
I am not my own
yet I am enslaved
to the idea
of Me and Mine

state lines
never seem to
get any closer
no matter how far
we go
whether to Fancy Gap
or Florida

Time and distance
outlive each other
so as never to
cross paths

Driving is
an eternal trip
on gas

Are you sure
you understand
your purpose
in my life
do you really know
why I'm on
your mind?

Maybe you're infatuated
with my presence
or the image
I convey

...nevermind
it's just my
delusions of grandeur
invading the walls
of this rubber room

I could've made something
from the nothing you give
but it seems best to invent
such imaginings
when they're unexpected
and uninvited
a verbal party crasher
for your vanity

Frayed nerves
bruise easily
and to think you thought
it might be different
on the other side...

All of life
is but a song
of victory and strife

A floating melody
over discordant harmony

The tale we tell
in our bleeding
throes of passion

Startled out of a dream
idle in the heat
of an indian summer
thinking on memories
long past

In my former life
I was a shadow
stalking
lurking
hiding from the presence
of the light

Caught by surprise
naked in the afternoon
waves pouring
awash on my skin
melting the fabric
of flesh
crumbling off
my tired bones
in sweetest agony

These thoughts
and more
drift lazily
behind my eyes
awaiting this
wondrous reflection

Does it matter anymore
that I seem to be
in love
with falling to pieces
whenever I can't stand up
to this struggle

Maybe if I ever thought
to stand
on legs that weren't mine
in strength
I could never find
I might realize
that you'd carry me
if I asked

Daddy will you hold me?

I'm tired of this fight

Sleep soft
today's cares
wash away
carried off
in the rising tide
of dreams afloat
in what may come
spirit whispers
dancing days
and starfields bloom
heaven waits
earth groans
trumpets rise
the turning tide
tomorrow slides
eyes wide
here we go again

blink

blink

eyes wide open
focus unclear
parched these lips
move I dare me
lost by touch
Is anybody out there?
Stick close
life is passing

Ideas echo
in the blink of
a thousand thoughts
flash burnt to the walls
of my mind
and speak on this surreality
I know all too well

Picasso slept here
Dali provided the interior
my insanity envelopes
them all

Enter at your own risk

Soaring in the skyline

embers burn the atmosphere

Fallout in the boiler

washed up on these

desert beaches

Nuclear Winter

settles in for a season

Alone in this metropolis

of permanent shadows...

Rain washed away
the sounds of an empty day
spoken with great unrest
rolling across the battered sea
creatures of the deep
venture forth in the absence of light
enchanted in the eye of the storm
wonder at the tears of God
grieving for his creation....

so much seems dependent
upon the persistence of time
that I wonder how this works into
our utmost sense of urgency
or can we just sit back and realize
what it takes to let it go and understand
how much we really need to
live by the spinning of the seconds
....or at least that's what they'd
like us to believe anyway

....feeling a fresh wind in the back of my mind......a breeze alight with the wishes and desires of our passion......daydreaming inside the weight of paradise realigned.......alive in the love that surrounds us.....

❖

...this is how my heart swells.....wrapped in the steady beating of this romance of our eyes....dwelling in the flames that dance between us....a steady heat that ebbs with the tide of emotion coursing through our fingertips.....and so I smile and know that I found myself alive the moment I said I love you...

❖

...speak soft as the colors bleed to nightfall and the whisper of an ancient forest........ears awash in the sounds of nymphs and satyrs dancing in the moonlight.....just a dream or a memory.......both are fading as the fire inside consumes the life denied...

❖

night skies twist and fade......burning in the eyes reflected by candlelight....sweet aromas filling the air as sweat glides across bodies entwined......lost in the ecstasy of touch and taste....lovers dance in secret rhythms.....trusting hearts and minds to the deepest needs....flowing in fluid motion....passion is a daydream best fulfilled at midnight...

bending close....ears tuned to the sounds of lovers breathing soft in the courts of slumber....wonder what she'd think if she knew I loved to watch her sleep....so peaceful...so fragile....a lonely vigil for the passing night...

wonder if the stars ever fall like we'd like them to....dancing in the arms of lightning that spiral against this night sky.....bleeding from their heavenly place......and I wonder if the sun would shine if I asked her to....warming this flesh that knows only cold.....but wondering never really gets me anywhere...

moonlight bathed two glistening bodies blending with the fire inside.......sparks hiss and pop as shadows flicker and dance in the eyes of voyeuristic animals.....mesmerized by the secret passions of this endless embrace....a melody fit for the secret life of the lovesong lost.....and found burning amidst us...

in this we say goodnight never dreaming of goodbye....walk easy in these pathways of dreams and memories...the morning sky will claim its passion and find me waiting on the outskirts...

starlight wondering at the ghost on the moon.....speak soft as not to wake this beauty at the gates of slumber....sparkles dancing in eyes that roam this darkness where our bodies tend to dwell at twilight.....wishing for the faceless orb dominating the evening sky to fall and be no more.....and so the story goes....lost and never known...

www.ingramcontent.com/pod-product-compliance
Lightning Source LLC
Chambersburg PA
CBHW031406040426
42444CB00005B/441